Heart Breathings

A Poetry Collection & Journal

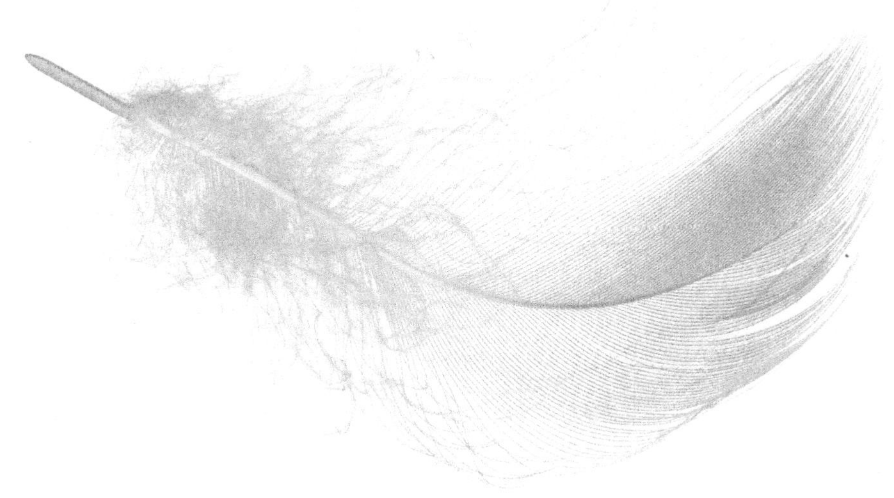

Lynz Burton

Dedication

for Darren and Keira
I love you both
I hope you know how special you are

Introduction

Hi there!
You have in your hands my humble poetry collection. Each poem
came to me during meditation or inspired by some of my
favourite teachers.

I've created a space for you to journal if you wish.

Read it however you feel comfortable.

From front to back, back to front, dip in and out.

From my heart to yours,
enjoy x

She was from social expectations and her
own high expectations

She was from the bubbling overwhelm and
bone-tired exhaustion

She was from bright coloured tulips, new
beginnings and spring solstice greetings

She was from loss, weakness, strength and
healing

She was from her ancestors, each fought
their own battles, passing their losses and
wins from their cells to hers

She was from children should be seen and
not heard, but live loud and proud

She was from the one that might have
been, the controller, the one that set her
free and standing on her own two feet

She refused to be from their opinions,
judgements, relationships that fizzed away
or crashed and burned

One day in a moment of awakening she
realised she was from mother nature, each
petal of each flower, the bird song, crickets
rubbing their wings together in the
bracken, acorns and high oak trees, the
blue sky, sun, moon, stars and calm water

She was from each season, autumn leaves,
crisp winter snow, bluebells in the spring,
a summer breeze

She was from the heart, loving, kind,
happy and content

She was from each breath that gave her life

She was from the energy of aliveness that
she could feel as she became still

She was, from now on, free!

By loving yourself

fully without conditions
you find inner peace

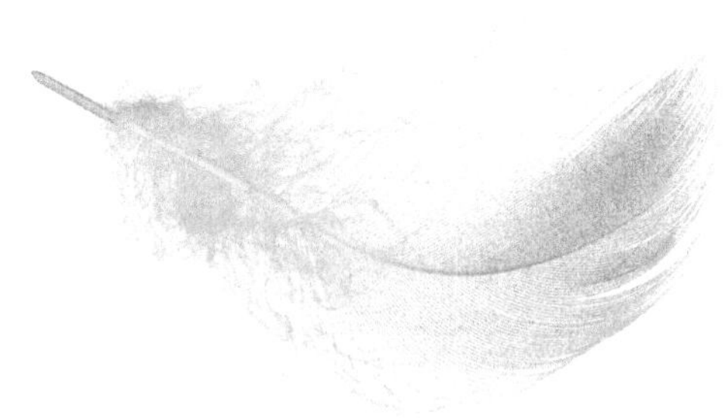

I came here for love

with a heartfelt
understanding
that sometimes
it wouldn't feel
so good

the broken and healing kind
two wings
of the
same bird
without one
I'd never
be able fly

times in the
tops of the trees
singing my sweet
love song

times
winds have nearly
blown me away

but
when the bough breaks
my heart has the strength
to heal and start again

Remember her

the part of you
that calls
for you to
wrap your arms
around her
hold her tight
and never let go

She accepts you

even if you can't

It's ok to

hide for a while
rest
feel
heal

but remember to
hide in
the heart
and not
the head

DATE:_____________

Mind asked body

for its hand in marriage
body said yes
mind relaxed
body softened
breath let go
heart skipped a beat
they lived
happily ever after

DATE:

Fearlessness resides

in the chambers of the heart
the door is open

DATE:

Please don't discard me

just because you think I'm weak
I've never skipped a beat

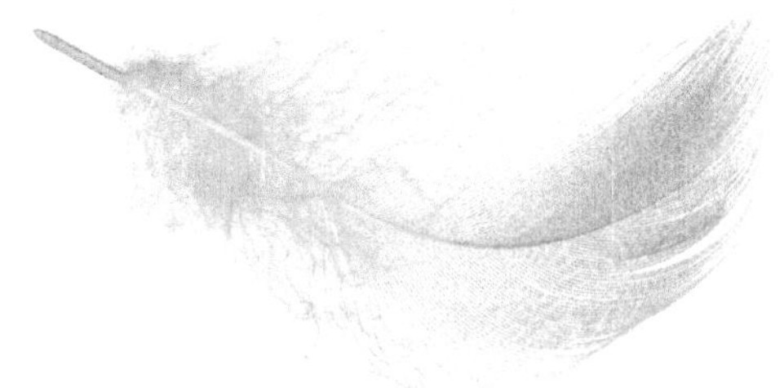

Listen to your heart

it's not afraid to
speak the truth

each beat is a message
from a guide within

DATE:___________

Sick and tired
of feeling
sick and tired

        hand on heart
          feeling heavy
            and dark

a single breath
a single wish
a desire for happiness

        heart whispers
              yes
        then fills the body
              with

Loving Kindness

DATE:_____________

I dedicate
my entire life
to those who have
broken me
and
those who have
helped me
piece myself
back together again

I love you
with every
breath
in my heart

without you all
such beauty
would never
have been
possible

Date:_____________

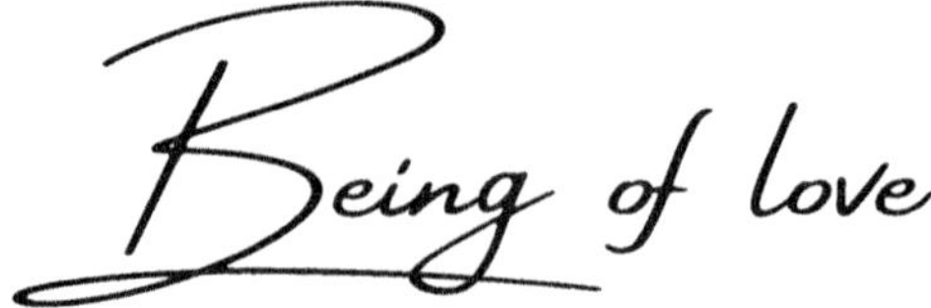

Being of love

I wish you could see you
the way I see you

a vision of beauty
stands before me

if you take your
eyes away
from every detail
you criticise
today
you will see you
the way I see you

a vision of love
sent from heaven above

if you just let go of
the thoughts
that self-destruct
the endless perfection
that's never enough

you will see you
the way I see you

I behold
a gentle soul
a vision of an angel

eyes filled with compassion
heart filled with love
don't you dare
write yourself off

look at yourself
open your eyes
dig deep my love
because what you think you see
is an elusion
the faults you feel
a false delusion

I see you the way I do
because
I see the truth

you see, I used to feel like you
but someone told me
to live a life of
integrity
to look at myself with love

it took some strength
to peel away the lies

but now I see me
the way I see you
and if I can find peace
you can too

She removed

her heart
from her chest

holding it tenderly
like a bird
with a broken wing

So small
in the palm of her hand

silently weeping
as she tended to the wounds

bathed it in warm soapy tears
of kindness

running her fingers
over familiar scars
cleaning cuts
she hadn't noticed before

removing thorns and gravel
from trips and falls
of years gone by

lifting it softly to her mouth
she whispered
"I've found you, I feel you, my love will heal
you"

I search for sunlight

under the moon and the stars
I can't find it there

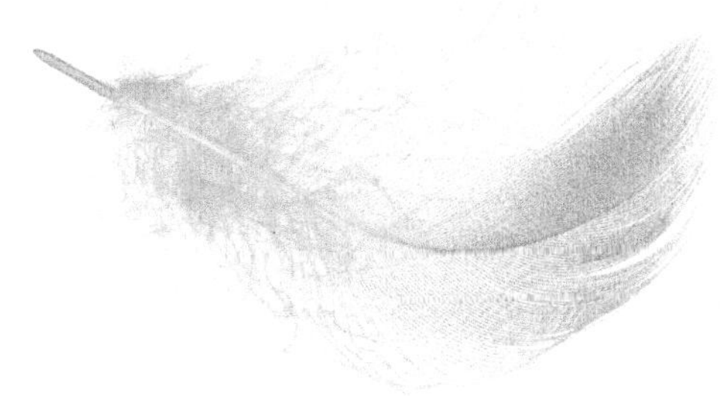

This won't last long you know

just a storm in a teacup
tides of peace come next

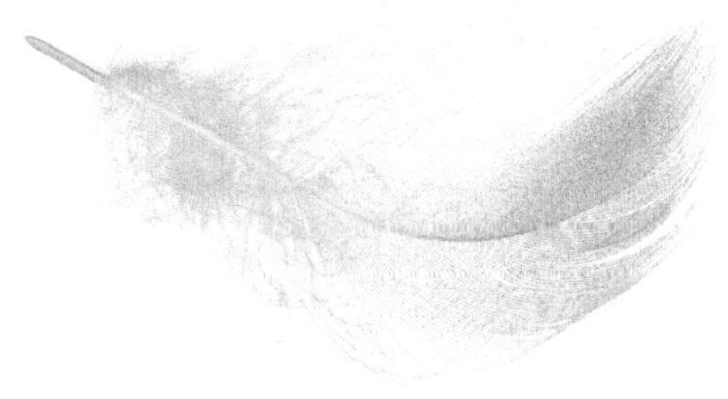

DATE:_________

Light and dark reside

inside space for cruel and kind
which one you decide

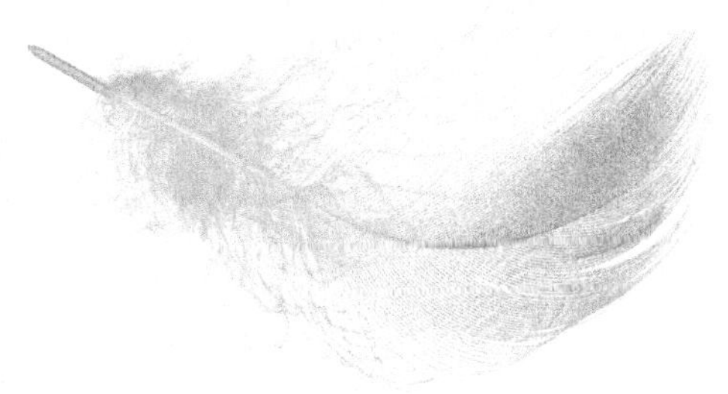

DATE:___________

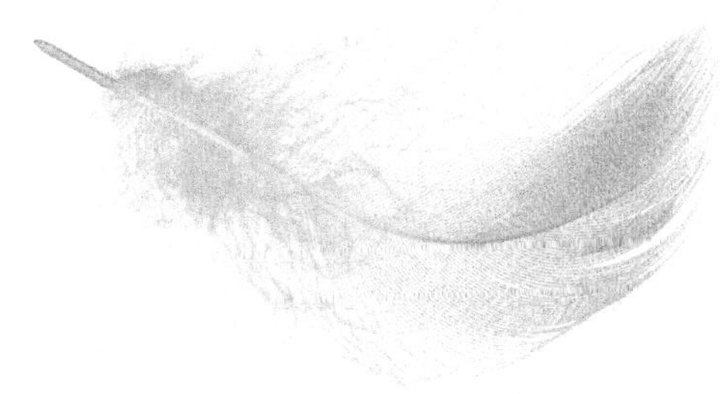

I'll leave the light on

said the moon to the night sky
you are safe with me

DATE:__________

When the past is heavy on your chest

when you find it hard to breathe
wrap your arms around yourself and whisper
I am at ease, I am at ease,
I am at ease

When your mind is struggling
when you feel you can't think straight
wrap your arms around yourself and whisper
it's ok, it's ok,
it's ok

When the future looks dark
when you feel you cannot see
wrap your arms around yourself and whisper
I am free, I am free,
I am free

When your emotions are overwhelming
when you can't escape the feelings
wrap your arms around yourself and whisper
I am healing, I am healing,
I am healing

When this moment feels lonely
when you don't want to be alone
I will wrap my arms around you, and whisper
you are home, you are home,
you are home

DATE:____________

Everything starts and ends with the breath
our most precious gift. given to us
at birth
and lasts only until
death

the gift of independence
as we enter the world
setting us free

a reminder that nothing lasts forever
and everything is subject to change

the breath is a spirit guide
showing you when to lean in
when to flow
when to hold back
when to let go

meet your breath where you are right now
breathe deep
feel it in your lungs
heart
pulsing through your veins

breathe deep
let every breath
between
life and death
be filled with
gentle
loving-kindness

breathe deep
a reminder that you are
alive
each breath holds
the possibility
that you can reach
your destiny

and truly be
everything
you have ever
wanted
to be

DATE:_____________

Feel the feet

each step of the way
one foot in front
of the other

feel the breath
each cycle
in and out
one breath
after another

feel the heart
lub dub
the rhythm
we can do this
together

When the tides

are calm
I stay

when the waves
try and wash me away
I stay

when the water
is clear
I stay

when the silt
fills each droplet
I stay

when the
movement
is rhythmical
and it makes
me sway
I stay

when the
sea bed
is untouchable
I stay

when
it's deserted
and bone dry
I stay

when it
quenches my
thirst
I stay

for I am
not separate
from the
the conditions

I am the container
I am the water
I am the stay

Date:____________

I seek shelter in love

storms happen it's part of life
know this too shall pass

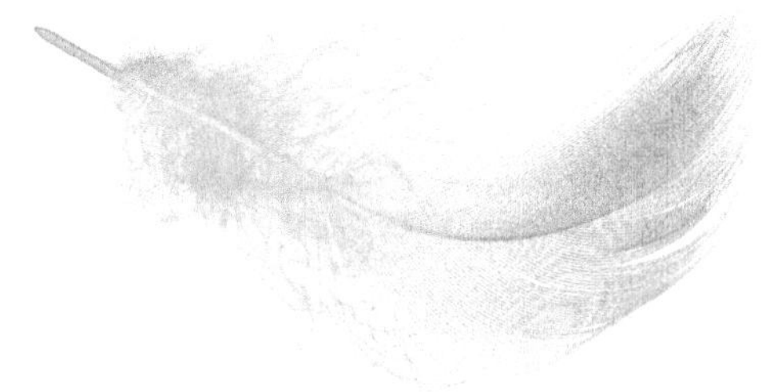

DATE:________

She'd been through so many storms
she had nothing left to lose

today she would dance
in the rain
soaking up whatever life had to offer
with
attitude
fortitude
and
gratitude

Date:_________

I pray to be
the space between
two thoughts

                                   I desire to be
                    the stillness between the
                              inhale and exhale

I wish to be
the silence between
each heartbeat

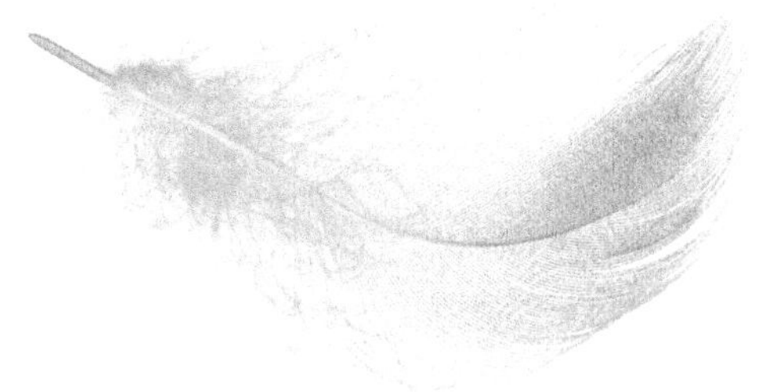

Date:_____________

Imagine your body
a home

In which room does your heart reside?

are the walls tatty and torn
old and worn
full of thorns, nails
and broken bricks?

is there a cage
instead of a door
past views on cheap newsprint
strewn all over the floor?

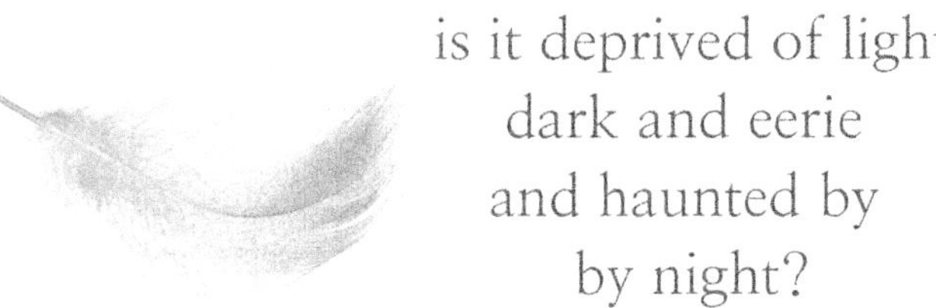

is it deprived of light
dark and eerie
and haunted by
by night?

is this really where you choose to rest
your most precious guest?

the joy of life is
nothing's set in stone
in each moment
you get to choose
how to decorate
your home

a room
fit for a heart
each brick
placed with love
clean walls covered in
breathtaking art

a 'welcome home' mat
sits at the foot of
every open door
plush fluffy carpets
feel more like clouds
than a floor

sun shines brightly
through
windows
little kisses of light

stars dance with the moon
while the heart sings
sweet, sweet love songs
in the heat of the night

a table
with flowers
fruit cake
and tea

pulling out a chair
heart opens
to serve
you for
all of eternity

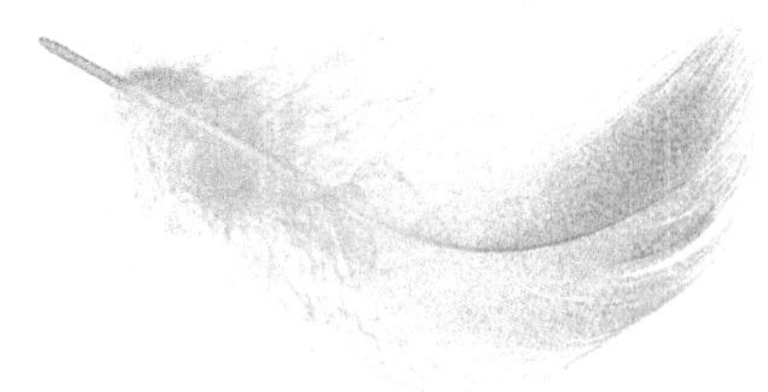

DATE:_________

My path is not enlightenment
it's awakening
peel the layers of delusion away slowly
I've been living under its veil for so long

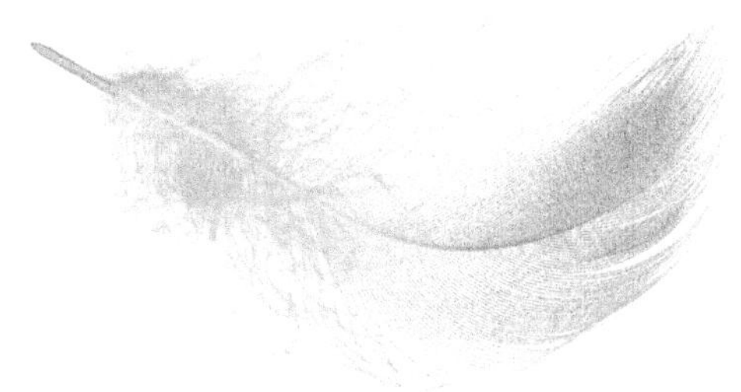

DATE:__________

Listening inwardly

eyes close
heart softens
breath sighs
throat opens
body relaxes
releasing a layer of tension
a moment of tender loving kindness

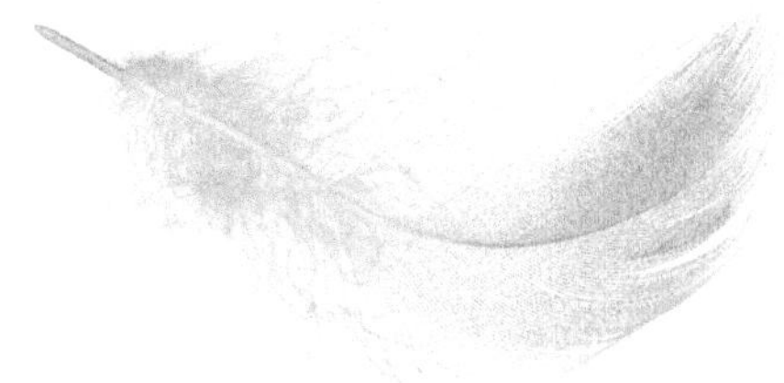

Date:_____________

Letting go
of what's
gripping you tight
in this
very
moment now

is a way of
of saying yes to life
of saying yes to death
and all that arises
in between

so, relax the body
surrender to what is

do what needs to be done
to let everything
become undone

hold the
suffering
and the
love
tenderly

make a vow to
live today
open to what may
with a heart of
equanimity

perhaps
this is
the key
to
life?

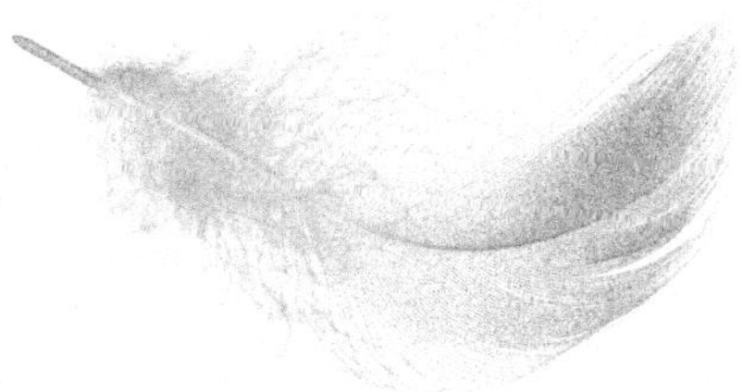

DATE:____________

In the moment she stopped
digging herself out of the rough like a precious
diamond
brushing herself off
holding herself high
to the light of her heart

The light caught her just right
she saw love
passion
humour
humility
beauty
and wisdom

she vowed to stop and look more often

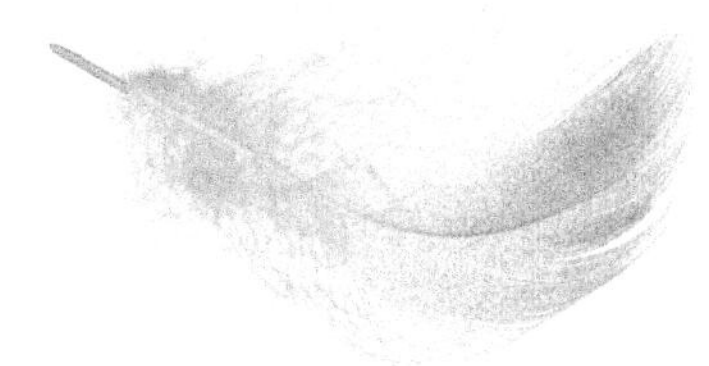

Date:_____________

Under everything

Under the noise
is a space, so still,
so quiet, it's peace

Under the burden
is a space, so still,
so quiet, it's love

Under the heartbreak
is a space, so still,
so quiet, it's love

Under everything you have ever believed about yourself,
is you,
it's beautiful

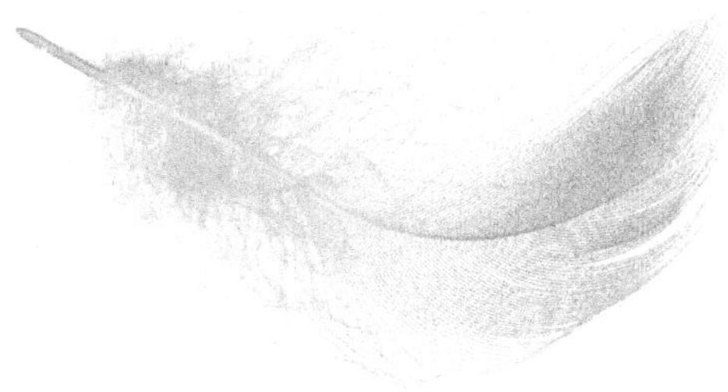

Date:______________

It's the little things

between the sunrise and sunset
sunset and sunrise

it's the little things
between the breath in and breath out

it's the little things
between the past and the future

it's the little things between
life and death

it's the little things
between my heart and yours
your heart and mine

how many things have been missed
being caught up in the mind
all the little things that make me feel truly alive

DATE:_____________

My heart is the home

I've always been longing for
warm, cosy and safe

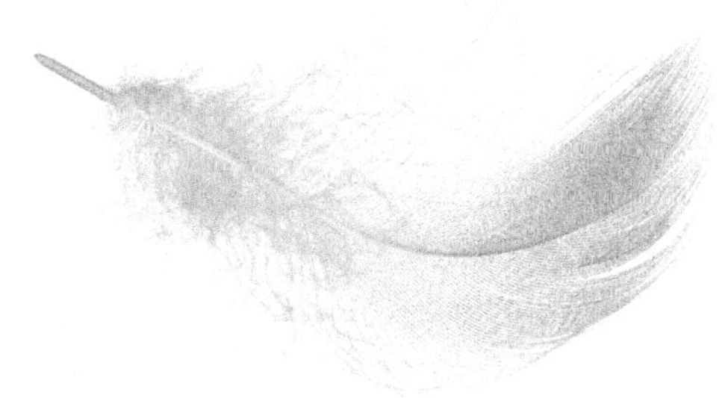

DATE:__________

Ease into stillness now
relax all the muscles that the body will allow

what lies beneath uncertainty
can you sense it?

a babbling brook of calm, a sea of tranquillity, inner
courage flowing through ocean after ocean after ocean

calm your inner waters by slowing the breath and
inviting a touch of gentle loving–kindness

soften the mind and relax the heart

allowing enough space for gratitude to spark

under the clutter that fills the space,
sound that fills the silence,
lies nothing but prepossessing nowness

all you need to do is ease into stillness now

Date:______________

I love you

(definition)
I can sing
your heart song
back to you
in the moments
you don't
feel strong

Date:_____________

I Love You

(meaning)
I can hold
my heart open
for us both
when yours
feels broken

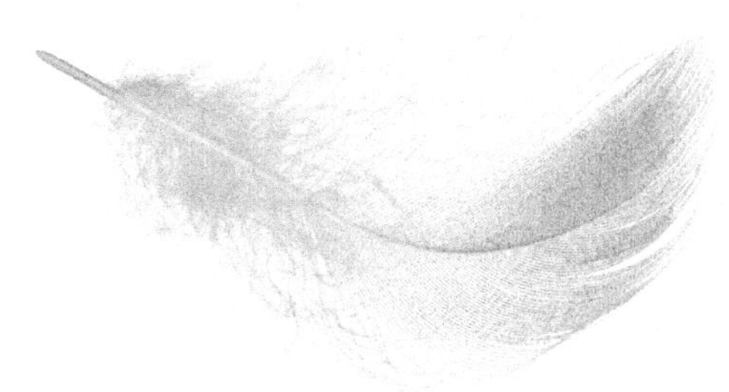

DATE:_________

I LOVE YOU

(description)
is when
our hearts
align as one
and all judgments
of separateness
are all but gone

Freedom to love comes

when kindness meets your heartache
asking for friendship

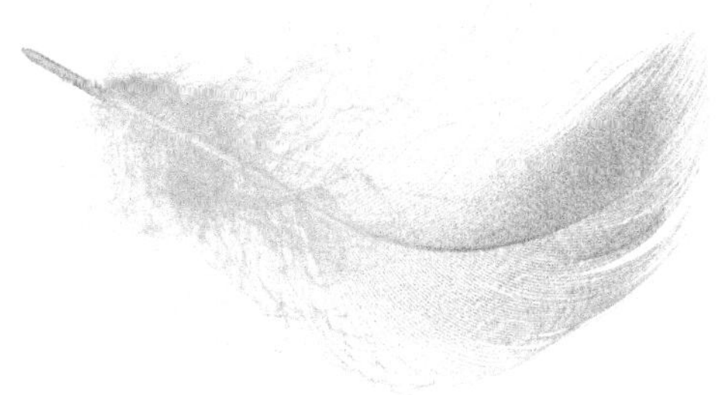

Date:_____________

I'm not afraid
of the thunder
fuelling the rain

I've weathered
more storms
than a teacup's
sustained

I put on my
waterproof coat
and dancing shoes
then sing with
my heart and soul
in tune with
natures
rhythm and blues

DATE:_____________

When the lights go out
the heart of the moon shines bright
stars gather in grace

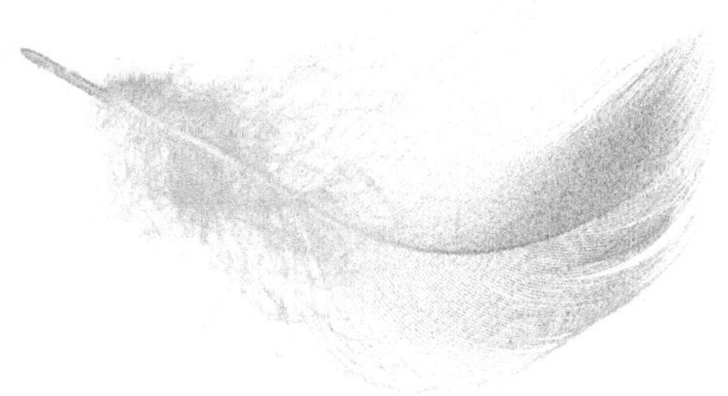

DATE:____________

Sun, rain, clouds and hail
knock at the door of our hearts
welcome all with love

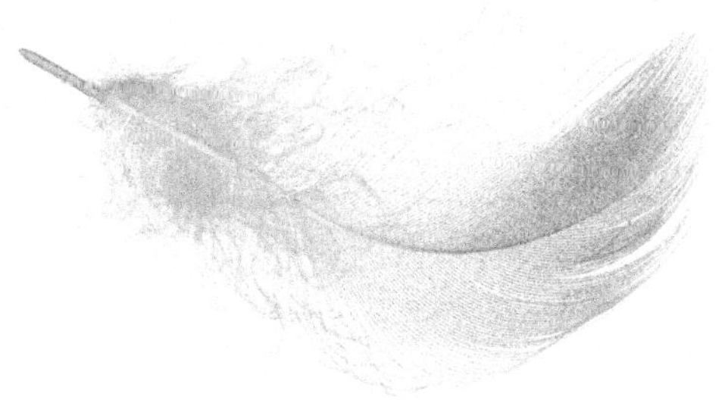

DATE:___________

Wild and wonderful

Butterfly wings and sunshine
You are beautiful

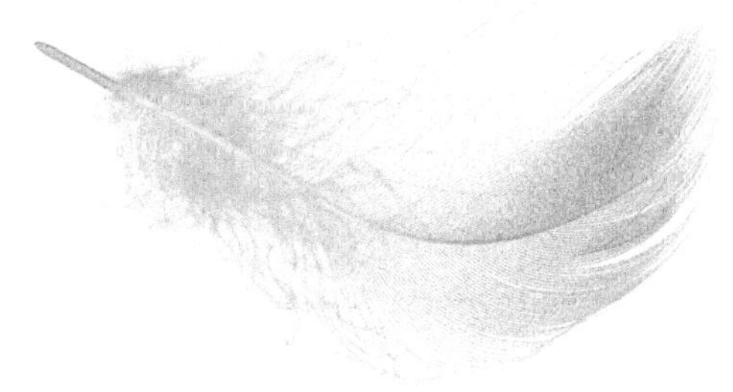

DATE:______________

My heart said to me

be the change you want to feel
I want to feel love

DATE:_____________

The mind asks the heart

"How can I love myself more"
Heart replies "feel me"

Date:_________

Broken from the start
and I was never
meant for this world
because you made me feel like I was
nothing
you took
love and respect
and replaced it with
shame, guilt and humiliation
you took everything
and I find it hard to believe
I wasn't broken from the start

– read it again from bottom to the top

Until we meet again
May you be happy
May you be well
May you be safe

Lynz Burton

Printed in Great Britain
by Amazon

62316574R00058